World Book's Animals of the World

Pinktoes
and Other Tarantulas

World Book, Inc.
a Scott Fetzer company
Chicago

Contents

What Is a Tarantula?

A tarantula is a type of hairy spider found in warm areas throughout the world. Tarantulas live on every continent except Antarctica.

Different kinds of tarantulas vary in size. The leg span for adult tarantulas can range from about ½ inch (1.25 centimeters) to more than 10 inches (25.5 centimeters) across.

There are about 800 to 900 known species, or kinds, of tarantulas (see page 65). Most species of tarantulas live in burrows in the ground. But some tarantulas are arboreal *(ahr BAWR ee uhl),* which means they live above the ground in trees, bushes, or other high places. Several species of arboreal tarantulas are called by the common name of pinktoe.

A pinktoe tarantula

7

What Do Tarantulas, Including Pinktoes, Look Like?

Tarantulas have a body that is divided into two main parts—the abdomen *(AB duh muhn)* and the cephalothorax *(SEHF uh loh THAWR aks* or *SEHF uh loh THOHR aks).*

The abdomen is the rounded part at the back of the tarantula that contains the animal's organs. The cephalothorax is at the front of the tarantula, and it contains the mouthparts, including the chelicerae *(kuh LIHS uh ree).* The chelicerae are above the spider's mouth opening, and the spider uses them to seize, crush, and kill its prey. Each chelicera ends in a sharp, hard, hollow fang. Eight eyes, eight legs, and two leglike structures called pedipalps are also connected to the cephalothorax.

One of the most popular kinds of tarantula kept as a pet is the pinktoe. As you might expect from its name, the tips of a pinktoe's legs are pink. A pinktoe has an abdomen that is usually black and a brown cephalothorax.

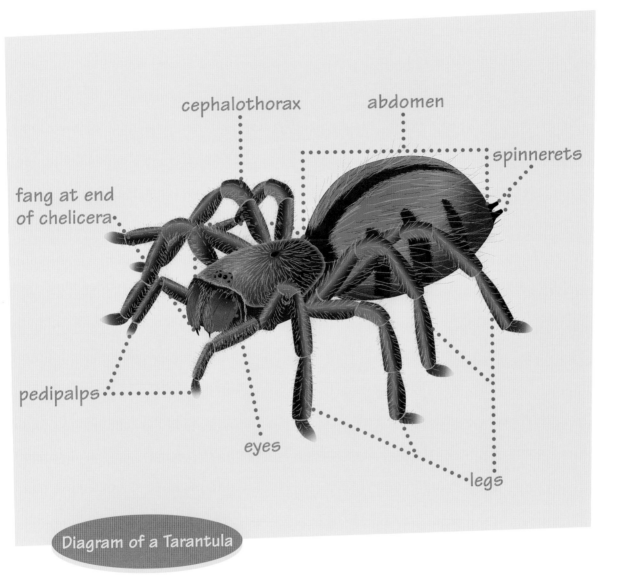

cephalothorax

abdomen

spinnerets

fang at end
of chelicera

pedipalps

eyes

legs

Diagram of a Tarantula

9

Where Do Pinktoes Live in the Wild?

Pinktoes live in tropical regions (areas near Earth's equator that have mostly warm temperatures the year around and plentiful rainfall). Pinktoes live in tropical areas of South America, Central America, and Mexico, and on some islands in the Caribbean Sea.

Many kinds of tarantulas live in burrows in the ground, but pinktoes are arboreal tarantulas. The word arboreal relates to trees, and pinktoes are called arboreal because they mostly live in trees.

Some kinds of pinktoes, however, live among plants—especially tall grasses—or in houses and other buildings.

A Brazilian blue pinktoe in the wild

11

What Kind of Personality Might a Pet Pinktoe Have?

A pet pinktoe does not have a personality in the same way that a pet dog or cat would. The pinktoe, like most other tarantulas, will probably spend most of its time hiding. It will climb to the top of the container it lives in, spin a hiding place from silk, and stay there. It may come out for feeding time, but it probably will not move around its container very much.

Still, different species of tarantulas do behave differently. Some species are very fast moving. Such tarantulas are quick to attack any "intruder" in their container, which could include the hand of the person trying to feed and care for them.

Pinktoes, however, are not usually aggressive. They are gentle, calm, slow moving, and even friendly. They rarely bite.

The gentle pinktoe

13

What Should You Look for When Choosing a Pinktoe ?

Finding a pet pinktoe should not be very hard. You can buy one from a pet store or from someone who raises tarantulas, such as a breeder. If you buy your tarantula from a breeder, he or she can teach you about the proper way to care for a pinktoe.

Try to buy a female pinktoe if you want your pet to be likely to live for a long time. Female tarantulas may live 20 years or more. Males usually live only a few years.

If you do not want to spend a lot of money on a pet tarantula, you may want to try a spiderling, or young spider. Spiderlings may be harder to feed, though, because they need to eat very small insects. But, with a spiderling, you can have the fun of watching your young pet grow and molt (see page 50) more frequently than an adult would.

BEWARE OF
SCORPION

Choosing a pet

15

What Does a Pinktoe Eat?

Like other tarantulas, pinktoes are completely carnivorous. This means that they eat only other animals and never eat plants. Pinktoes mostly eat insects. They do not chase and capture their prey. Instead, they wait quietly near their home (see page 20) for prey to come to them.

A pinktoe uses its chelicerae (see pages 8 and 9) to grab insects that pass by its home. Once a pinktoe has a grip on its prey, it stabs its prey with fangs. Poison, called venom, flows through the spider's fangs and into its victim. The poison stuns the animal so that it cannot fight back. Then, the pinktoe sprays digestive juice over the prey, turning it into a thin "soup." Spiders have mouthparts that can be formed into something like a straw. This allows the spider to suck up its liquid meal.

The time it takes a tarantula to consume a meal depends on the size of the prey. A cricket may be turned to liquid and sucked up in an hour. A full-grown mouse might take 24 hours. When the pinktoe is finished eating, all that is left of the prey is a small ball of remains.

A pinktoe with prey

17

How Should You Feed Your Pinktoe?

If you have an adult pinktoe, it should be fed once a week. If you have a younger pet that is still growing, feed it twice a week or more. Crickets, cockroaches, and grasshoppers are all good food for pinktoes. You can also feed your pinktoe mealworms. Do not, however, feed your pet insects that you capture yourself. Insects you capture may have pesticides (bug-killing poisons) on them. Also, do not feed your pinktoe any insect that may be dangerous to your pet, such as ants, wasps, and stinkbugs.

You can buy crickets or other insects to feed your pinktoe at a pet store. When your pinktoe has finished eating, remove the remains of the meal or any uneaten food right away.

A pinktoe is offered a cricket

19

Do Pinktoes Spin?

Spiders spin silk to make many kinds of structures. Like all spiders, pinktoes spin silk to create a home and to make an egg sac (see page 30). Unlike many spiders, however, pinktoes do not spin silk to make webs for catching prey.

Pinktoes and other tree-dwelling tarantulas spin their homes in the shape of a tube they can hide in or in the shape of a small hammock they can rest in.

Other kinds of tarantulas live underground. These tarantulas dig burrows for their home. These tarantulas do not spin webs to catch prey, but they do line their burrows with silk that they have spun. They may also leave a few strands of silk trailing out from the burrow's opening. If an animal crosses or touches this silk strand, the tarantula is alerted and knows to come out and look for a meal.

A pinktoe tarantula in its silken home

21

Where Does a Spider's Silk Come From?

With all spiders, including tarantulas, their silk comes out of two pairs of organs at the back end of the abdomen. These silk-producing organs are called spinnerets (see page 9).

Spinnerets work something like the fingers of a hand. Spiders use their spinnerets to spin silk into a very thin strand or a thick, wide strand.

Spider silk is made up of protein that forms in a spider's silk glands. Spiders make different kinds of silk for different uses. Some silk dries once it is outside a spider's body. Other kinds of silk stay sticky. Spider silk cannot be dissolved in water and is the strongest natural fiber we know of.

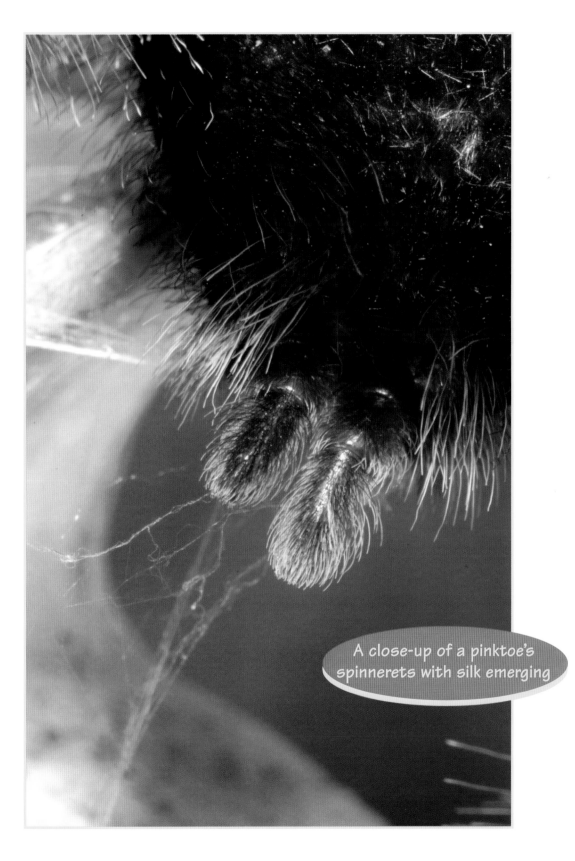

A close-up of a pinktoe's spinnerets with silk emerging

Where Should a Pet Pinktoe Be Kept?

You can keep a pinktoe in an aquarium *(uh KWAIR ee uhm)* tank, a plastic container, or a homemade container. Your pinktoe's home needs a tight-fitting cover to keep the spider from escaping.

Your pinktoe can stay healthy only if it is kept warm and moist. A temperature from 72 to 79 °F (22 to 26 °C) is good. Use vermiculite—a type of flaky, layered mineral—on the bottom of the container to hold moisture. Mist the tank often to provide moisture for your pet to drink. Tree-dwelling spiders like drinking water off the sides of the tank better than out of a bowl of water.

Because pinktoes are tree dwellers, give your pet a container tall enough to allow it to climb. For a full-grown pinktoe, a container that is 8 to 10 inches wide, 8 to 10 inches deep, and 12 inches high (20 to 25 centimeters wide, 20 to 25 centimeters deep, and 30 centimeters high) is fine. Provide a small tree branch that your pinktoe can climb on and attach its silky home to.

A pinktoe in
its container

Can More
Than One Pinktoe
Live Together?

As a general rule, it is not a good idea to keep more than one tarantula in the same container. Tarantulas will eat their own kind. If two tarantulas are kept in the same cage, one of them will almost certainly become dinner for the other.

Pinktoes have no need for companionship. To avoid all risk of one pinktoe killing the other, it is best to give each its own container.

Tarantulas should not share a container

Which Is Bigger, the Male or the Female?

In general, female tarantulas tend to be larger than males. There are several possible reasons for this. One is that the female's body stores nutrients used to form eggs. Another reason is that her body has special reproductive organs. She also has larger glands for spinning silk.

Male tarantulas may look daintier than females. They usually have smaller bodies. Their fangs are also thinner and narrower than those of females. The legs of a male tarantula are longer and thinner than those of a female.

A female (left) and male Mexican redknee

What Is a Spiderling?

A young dog is a puppy. A young spider is a spiderling.

For pinktoe spiderlings to hatch, first, the male gets ready for mating by spinning a small net of silk. Next, he releases sperm from his body onto the silk. Then he collects the sperm in special organs in the tips of his pedipalps. When he is ready to mate, he approaches the female. If she is ready, she allows him to place his sperm into her body.

The female pinktoe lays eggs several weeks or even months after mating. First, she spins a thick net of silk. Then, she lays eggs inside the silk. The eggs combine with the stored sperm as they pass out of the female's body. She lays between 50 and 125 eggs. When she is done, she wraps the silk around the eggs to create an egg sac.

Pinktoe spiderlings hatch from their eggs about 7 to 8 weeks later as tiny, fully mobile spiders.

Two-day-old pinktoe spiderlings

Why Does a Pinktoe Have Such "Hairy" Legs?

Like all tarantulas, pinktoes have hairs, called setae *(SEE tae* or *SEE tee)*, all over their legs and body.

Pinktoes use their setae for many purposes. Setae on the legs are used to sense vibrations in the air and on the ground. Thick mats of setae on the feet allow pinktoes to climb up smooth surfaces with ease. Other types of setae on the feet allow the animal to taste its food, while setae around the mouth filter the food.

Many tarantulas, including pinktoes, have special setae that help them defend themselves. These are called urticating *(UR tuh kay ting)* hairs. Urticating hairs are sharp, with very tiny barbs, or hooks, at the end of them. These hairs dig into the skin, and even the eyes, of an enemy, causing burning and irritation. A pinktoe must brush against an enemy to drive the urticating hairs into the enemy's skin. But other tarantulas can use their legs to kick hairs off and throw them at an enemy.

A close-up of a pinktoe's setae

Are Tarantulas Venomous?

Luckily, pinktoes rarely bite. If they do, their bite—like that of most other tarantulas—is only mildly venomous (poisonous). Some people compare a tarantula bite with a bee sting. Tarantula venom is dangerous only to people who are allergic to it. There are no known cases of a person dying from a tarantula bite. However, a tarantula's bite can be painful, and its fangs can cause nasty puncture wounds. If you are bitten, let an adult know immediately.

Treat a tarantula bite like any other animal bite. Wash the bite with soap and warm water. Put on an antiseptic ointment and a bandage, if you need one.

It is more likely that you may get stuck with your pinktoe's urticating hairs—the bristly spines on its abdomen. This can be very uncomfortable. Use tweezers to remove the hairs from your skin. If hairs should get into your eyes or nose, see a doctor.

A tarantula in
an attack posture
shows its fangs

Can a Tarantula Be Held?

Most experts do not recommend holding any tarantula. It is dangerous to pick up or touch a tarantula from any of the fast, aggressive species. Not even an experienced tarantula keeper would do this.

Although pinktoes and other gentle tarantulas are usually calm, they can bite. The spider's urticating hairs also can cause an uncomfortable skin rash or more serious harm to the eyes and nostrils.

Holding a tarantula can be dangerous to the spider as well. Tarantulas have fragile bodies. Dropping a tarantula could injure its abdominal area, which could be fatal to your pet. Always be gentle and careful when you move your tarantula. You may gently lift the tarantula with tongs. Or, you may use a paintbrush with a long handle and soft bristles to carefully place the tarantula into a container.

Safely handling a tarantula

What Are Some Other Gentle Tarantulas?

Besides pinktoes, there are a number of other mild-mannered tarantula species. These tarantulas include the Mexican redleg, the Mexican redrump, the Mexican redknee, the Chilean rose, and the curlyhair. All of these are ground-dwelling tarantulas from North or South America. They all make good pets for anyone—even a beginner—interested in having a spider for a pet. One downside of all these gentle tarantulas is that they, unlike pinktoes, do have the ability to throw off urticating hairs.

Mexican redlegs and Mexican redknees are beautiful black spiders with either orange or orange-red stripes around their legs. Mexican redrumps are black with a red abdomen. Curlyhairs have orange hairs on their legs and abdomen. Chilean roses can have a gray undercoat with gray and beige, pink, or copper-colored hairs.

A Chilean rose
tarantula

Which Tarantulas Might Not Make Such Good Pets?

Even though certain types of tarantulas might be available for sale as pets, they may be difficult for people who are new to caring for spiders.

For example, some species have special or unusual needs that make them harder to care for. The Trinidad chevron, which needs very high humidity, is one such spider.

Other difficult tarantulas include the Brazilian salmon, the Goliath birdeater, the king baboon tarantula of Africa, the Sri Lankan ornamental, the cobalt blue, and the Australian tarantulas (also called whistling or barking spiders). Large size, beauty, or interesting behaviors may make all these tarantulas tempting pets, but they are recommended only for experienced spider owners.

All of the tarantulas mentioned above are aggressive and fast moving. The venom of the king baboon tarantula is also more dangerous to humans than the venom of most other tarantulas.

A Trinidad chevron

41

What Is the Biggest Tarantula?

The world's largest tarantula is the Goliath birdeater tarantula.

This tarantula lives in the rain forests of South America. Its leg span can be more than 10 inches (25 centimeters)—that is about the size of a small dinner plate.

When it feels threatened, the Goliath birdeater rubs the bristles on its legs together to make a loud hissing noise (see page 54). This noise is called stridulation *(STRIHJ uh LAY shuhn)*. The Goliath has other defensive moves as well. It can rear up on its hind legs to intimidate an enemy, and it also throws its urticating hairs (see page 32) when it feels afraid.

Although it is called "birdeater," this tarantula's diet is not limited to birds. The Goliath birdeater also eats frogs, toads, lizards, mice, and small snakes.

A Goliath birdeater

What Are Some of the Smallest Tarantulas?

The smallest known tarantulas grow only from about ½ inch to about 1 inch (about 1.25 to 2.5 centimeters) across.

Some of these dwarf tarantulas are found in the genus (see page 65) called *Cyriocosmus* from Central and South America. Some *Cyriocosmus* tarantulas are beautifully patterned with red and black markings.

Another dwarf tarantula is *Aphonopelma paloma,* a tarantula from Arizona. This species grows to about ½ inch (1 centimeter) across.

An Aphonopelma
tarantula

Which Tarantulas Are Champion Diggers?

Many species of tarantula live in burrows in the ground. But some tarantulas dig deeper than others.

Australian tarantulas, also called whistling or barking spiders, live in hot areas. They make a noise that sounds like whistling or barking when disturbed. These tarantulas dig burrows that are 1 to 3 feet (0.3 to 0.9 meter) deep. That far under the ground, it is cool and damp. Australian tarantulas will sometimes cover the opening of their burrow with silk to keep the moisture in. They may also build a mound of soil around the burrow entrance, which they cover with silk. The silk collects dew and raindrops for the spider to drink. The mound also keeps water from flooding the burrow.

King baboon tarantulas also dig deep burrows. Their burrows are more than 2 feet (0.6 meters) deep. These large tarantulas live in the grasslands of east-central Africa.

Cobalt blue tarantulas of Southeast Asia also dig large tunnels in the floor of the tropical forest.

46

An Australian tarantula at the entrance to its burrow

What Are the Enemies of Tarantulas in the Wild?

Tarantulas must face a number of dangerous enemies. Birds, frogs and toads, lizards, snakes, and skunks and certain other mammals all dine on tarantulas. Some insects also prey on tarantulas.

One well-known enemy of the tarantula is the *Pepsis* wasp, often called the tarantula hawk. This wasp uses a tarantula as a kind of nursery and cafeteria for its young.

An adult female *Pepsis* wasp attacks and stings a tarantula. The wasp's venom paralyzes the tarantula but does not kill it. The wasp lays an egg on the spider's body. An undeveloped form of the wasp, called a larva, hatches from the egg. The larva then burrows into the spider and begins to eat it. The larva feeds on the tarantula until the tarantula dies. Slowly, the larva turns into an adult form of a wasp.

Several other types of wasps prey on tarantulas or other spiders in this way.

A *Pepsis* wasp
confronts a tarantula

How Does a Tarantula Grow?

A tarantula's skeleton is on the outside of its body. This type of skeleton is called an exoskeleton.

An exoskeleton cannot grow larger. So, when a tarantula's insides get too big for its exoskeleton, the exoskeleton splits and falls away. The spider then develops a new exoskeleton. This process is called molting. Young spiders molt often as they grow. Adult females molt about once a year. Adult males rarely molt.

Your pet tarantula usually will stop eating a few days before it begins molting. The exoskeleton will split around the edge of the body and separate from the body. The spider then has to pull its legs carefully out of the old exoskeleton.

Do not touch your spider during its molt. Also, do not put any food—and especially no live insects—into your spider's container when it is molting. A molting spider is defenseless and fragile.

A tarantula (left) beside its recently molted exoskeleton

exoskeleton

Does a Tarantula Enjoy a Swim?

Tarantulas do not like getting wet. They can sense even tiny amounts of water with their legs. They try to avoid getting into water above their head. Nevertheless, arboreal tarantulas sometimes accidentally fall into ponds and streams from overhanging tree branches.

A tarantula will usually float if it falls into water. Tiny air bubbles trapped between the setae (see page 32) on a tarantula's body and legs keep it afloat. The tarantula can then swim to dry land by paddling with its front pair of legs.

Tarantulas are also waterproof. When they climb out of the water, they are perfectly dry.

52

A Peruvian pinktoe
in water

Are Tarantulas Noisy?

Many kinds of tarantulas can make noises when they are frightened or upset. This noise is called stridulating. Stridulating sounds like hissing. Different species of tarantulas make stridulating noises by rubbing different parts of their body against one another. The body parts used for stridulating include the legs, chelicerae, and pedipalps (see pages 8 and 9).

Tarantulas often stridulate while rising up on their back legs (see page 35). They strike with their front legs and show their fangs. Often, these actions frighten an attacker away.

legs

chelicerae

legs

pedipalps

legs

Body parts used for stridulation

55

Can Tarantulas Act?

Many people think tarantulas are scary and creepy. So, it is not surprising that filmmakers have used tarantulas in many horror, adventure, and even comedy films. Many science-fiction films, such as *Tarantula* (1955), have also featured large, scary spiders.

Mexican redknee tarantulas were used in the adventure film *Raiders of the Lost Ark* (1981). In one scene, at least 40 of these tarantulas swarmed over actors Harrison Ford and Alfred Molina. The people who handle the tarantulas used in such modern movies as *Raiders of the Lost Ark* are called spider wranglers. These wranglers work to get spiders to do the things the director desires. For example, spider wranglers might use thin vibrating wires, blow dryers, or slippery furniture-polish to help guide a spider's movements. As is often the case with scenes involving animals, sometimes a director must shoot a scene many times to finally catch a tarantula "following direction" on film.

A scene from the
1955 film *Tarantula*

57

What Are Some Common Signs of Illness in Tarantulas?

The most common problems in pet tarantulas are dehydration and wounds. In a tarantula, signs of dehydration—the loss of water from the body—include slow movement and a shriveled appearance.

Wounds are serious problems for tarantulas because their hemolymph (spider blood) does not clot (thicken) and stop the bleeding as human blood usually does. One possible treatment for a tarantula wound is to brush on something that will cover the wound and then dry hard, like the "liquid bandages" sold in drugstores for people. For a wound to a spider's abdomen, brush the wounded area with Superglue. To treat a tarantula wound, ask an adult for help.

Tarantulas are also very easily injured while they are molting. If a tarantula gets stuck in its old exoskeleton (see pages 50 and 51) during a molt, it could die.

58

A tarantula at a veterinary office

59

What Are Your Responsibilities as an Owner?

You are responsible for providing your tarantula with good food and a safe, clean, comfortable living space. You have to make sure to keep your tarantula's cage at the right temperature and humidity. Make sure the air in your tarantula's container is moist enough for your type of tarantula. Species that are native to desert areas need less moisture than species from rain-forest environments.

Protect your tarantula by handling it very carefully—or not at all. If your tarantula is injured, you must get an adult to help you treat the injury. Guard your pet against falls. Falling even a few feet can be dangerous for a tarantula.

Your female tarantula can live for 20 years or more, so be ready to make a long-lasting commitment to her care. If you can no longer care for your tarantula, find it a new home where it will be well cared for. You must not turn it loose.

A pinktoe

Tarantula Fun Facts

→ A female Mexican redknee tarantula can produce as many as 1,000 eggs at one time.

→ At least two species of tarantulas share their burrows with a certain type of frog. Scientists do not know exactly why, but they think the frogs may eat ants that bother the spider.

→ Scientists have discovered that the venom of certain tarantulas may be able to help stop potentially fatal muscle contractions that happen in humans after having a heart attack.

→ Mexican redknee tarantulas were once the most popular pet tarantula species. But they became scarce in the wild because people captured too many of them to sell as pets. Now, this tarantula is protected by the Mexican government.

Glossary

arboreal Living in or among trees.

burrow A hole dug in the ground by an animal for refuge or shelter. Also, to dig a hole in the ground.

carnivorous Feeding on meat.

chelicera One of a pair of structures near the mouth of a spider, which it uses to seize and kill its prey (plural, chelicerae).

dehydration In living things, to be in need of water.

exoskeleton The hard outer shell that covers and protects the bodies of arthropods (a large group of animals that includes spiders).

gland An organ in the body that separates materials from the blood and changes them into some substance for use in the body, or into a product to be released from the body, such as spider silk.

molt To shed old shell, skin, feathers, or other body coverings.

pedipalp One of a pair of short, leglike structures near the mouth and fangs of spiders.

prey Animals that are hunted and eaten by other animals. Also, to hunt or kill for food.

protein A large, complex molecule that forms a necessary part of the cells of animals and plants.

seta In spiders, a sensitive hair that serves as an organ of touch and smell. Some hairs pick up vibrations from the ground or air, others detect chemicals in the environment (plural, setae).

sperm The fluid of a male that fertilizes the eggs of the female.

spiderling A young spider.

spinneret The organ spiders use to spin silk.

stridulate To make a shrill, grating sound by rubbing together parts of the body.

venom The poison of some snakes, spiders, scorpions, lizards, and similar animals. Venom is injected into their prey by biting or stinging.

63

Index

(**Boldface** indicates a photo or illustration.)

For more information about Pinktoes and Other Tarantulas, try these resources:

The Tarantula Scientist, by Sy Montgomery, Houghton Mifflin, 2004

Tarantulas and Other Arachnids, by Samuel D. Marshall, Barron's Educational Series, 2nd edition, 2001

Uncover a Tarantula: Take a Three-Dimensional Look Inside a Tarantula!, by David George Gordon, Silver Dolphin Books, 2004

http://www.discover.com/issues/feb-04/features/stalking-spiders/?page=1

http://www.entomology.cornell.edu/SpiderOutreach/Tarantulas.html

http://jrscience.wcp.muohio.edu/downloads/naturalhistorytarantulas.pdf

Tarantula Classification

Scientists classify animals by placing them into groups. The animal kingdom is a group that contains all the world's animals. Phylum, class, order, and family are smaller groups. Each phylum contains many classes. A class contains orders, an order contains families, and a family contains genuses. One or more species belong to each genus. Each species has its own scientific name. (The abbreviation "spp." after a genus name indicates that a group of species from a genus is being discussed.) Here is how the animals in this book fit into this system.

Animals with jointed legs and their relatives (Phylum Arthropoda)
Arachnids (Class Arachnida)
Spiders (Order Araneae)

Tarantulas and their relatives (Infraorder Mygalomorphae)

Tarantulas (Family Theraphosidae)

Common pinktoe	*Avicularia avicularia*
Brazilian blue pinktoe	*Avicularia geroldi*
Peruvian pinktoe	*Avicularia urticans*
Mexican redknee	*Brachypelma smithi*
Mexican redleg	*Brachypelma emilia*
Mexican redrump	*Brachypelma vagans*
Curlyhair	*Brachypelma albopilosum*
King baboon	*Citharischius crawshayi*
Chilean rose	*Grammostola rosea*
Cobalt blue	*Haplopelma lividum*
Brazilian salmon	*Lasiodora parahybana*
Sri Lankan ornamental	*Poecilotheria fasciata*
Trinidad chevron	*Psalmopoeus cambridgei*
Goliath birdeater	*Theraphosa blondi*

Australian tarantulas, or whistling or barking spiders . . . . *Phlogiellus* (unnamed species), *Selenocosmia* spp., *Selenotholu foelschei, Selenotypus plumipes*

Dwarf tarantulas . . . . *Aphonopelma paloma, Cyriocosmus* spp.

Editor in Chief: Paul A. Kobasa
Supplementary Publications: Lisa Kwon, Christine Sullivan, Scott Thomas
Research: Mike Barr, Timothy J. Breslin, Cheryl Graham, Barbara Lightner, Loranne Shields
Graphics and Design: Kathy Creech, Sandra Dyrlund, Charlene Epple, Tom Evans
Permissions: Janet Peterson
Indexing: David Pofelski
Prepress and Manufacturing: Anne Dillon, Carma Fazio, Anne Fritzinger, Steven Hueppchen,
    Tina Ramirez
Writer: Lisa Klobuchar

For information about other World Book publications, visit our Web site at
http://www.worldbook.com or call 1-800-WORLDBK (967-5325).

For information about sales to schools and libraries, call 1-800-975-3250 (United States);
1-800-837-5365 (Canada).

World Book, Inc.
233 N. Michigan Avenue
Chicago, IL 60601
U.S.A.

Library of Congress Cataloging-in-Publication Data
Pinktoes and other tarantulas.
    p. cm. -- (World Book's animals of the world)
    Summary: "An introduction to Pinktoes and Other Tarantulas,
Presented in a highly illustrated, question and answer format.
Features include fun facts, glossary, resource list, index, and
scientific classification list"--Provided by publisher.
Includes bibliographical references and index.
  ISBN-13: 978-0-7166-1332-9
  ISBN-10: 0-7166-1332-8
  1. Tarantulas--Juvenile literature. I. World Book, Inc. II.
Series.
QL458.42.T5P56 2007
595.4'4--dc22
                            2006017322
Printed in Malaysia
1 2 3 4 5 6 7 8 09 08 07 06

Picture Acknowledgments: Cover: © Brian P. Kenney, Animals Animals; © Tom McHugh, Photo Researchers; © Michael Ready, Norbert Wu Productions; © Justin Sullivan, Getty Images.

© Dominique Braud, Animals Animals 3, 45; © Corbis/Underwood & Underwood 57; © Will and Lissa Funk 15, 59; © Brian P. Kenney, Animals Animals 11; © Tom McHugh, Photo Researchers 51; © Carolyn A. McKeone 27; © Claus Meyer, Minden Pictures 7; © John Mitchell, Photo Researchers 43; © Mark Moffett, Minden Pictures 17, 49, 53; © Reg Morrison, Auscape International 4, 47; © Michael Ready, Norbert Wu Productions 13, 19, 23, 25, 33, 37, 55, 61; © Justin Sullivan, Getty Images 39; © Nick Upton, Nature Picture Library 41; © Rick C. West 5, 21, 29, 31; © Frank B. Yuwono, Shutterstock 5, 35.

Illustrations: WORLD BOOK illustrations by John Fleck 9.

Pinktoes

and Other Tarantulas